DEMCO

The Legend *of the* Teddy Bear

By Frank Murphy
Illustrated by Gijsbert van Frankenhuyzen

Sleeping Bear Press

In memory of my mother.

— Gijsbert van Frankenhuyzen

*For my best friend and partner in life and writing, Debbie.
And to the everlasting memory of my mom, Kathleen Murphy.*

— Frank Murphy

Sleeping Bear Press
310 North Main Street
P.O. Box 20
Chelsea, MI 48118
www.sleepingbearpress.com

Printed and bound in Canada.

10 9 8 7 6 5 4 3 2 1

Library of Congress Cataloging-in-Publication Data on file.
ISBN: 1-58536-013-9

AUTHOR'S NOTE

A legend is a story created about a certain person, place, or thing. Many legends are based on fiction, which means they are not necessarily true. But the story of Theodore Roosevelt refusing to shoot that bear, Clifford Berryman's cartoon, and the Michtom's creation of the first teddy bears is based on fact.

Although many may first associate Theodore Roosevelt with the lending of his name to our country's favorite toy, there is so much more to this great man. He lived life to the fullest. He loved to read—reading two or three books in a day! He read ghost stories at night to his six children in the White House after pillow fights, wrestling, and hide-and-seek games.

Theodore Roosevelt was the first president to own a car, ride in an airplane, and dive in a submarine! He loved animals so much that he allowed the largest collection of pets ever in the White House. Dogs, kittens, flying squirrels, kangaroo rats, birds, and even a pony ran wild through the halls of the White House.

Theodore also left many lasting accomplishments. He published many books and essays and began the building of the Panama Canal. But perhaps most impressive, he saved millions of acres of public land by promoting the National Parks and National Forest systems. If it weren't for Theodore, today we might not have many of our natural resources, wildlife preserves, or national parks such as the Grand Canyon. Teddy Roosevelt truly stands as one of this country's greatest leaders.

I would like to thank Wallace Dailey, Curator of the Theodore Roosevelt Collection at the Harvard College Library, for his assistance. The Legend of the Teddy Bear has been retold here preserving as much of the factual history as possible, while crafting fictional details to add to many of the unknown elements of the history involved. Today there is a historical marker that points out the site where Theodore Roosevelt refused to shoot that bear!

Finally, I'd like to thank Denise Bryngelson for her meticulous fact-checking and Heather Hughes, my editor, for believing in this story from the start.

— Frank Murphy

ILLUSTRATOR'S ACKNOWLEDGMENTS

To illustrate my books, I use live models to act out the scenes of the stories. *The Legend of the Teddy Bear* was especially challenging because there were many diverse characters to paint. I want to thank Ashley and Kelsey Rohan-Olsen for spending several hours in my studio holding teddy bears in a hundred different poses. Thanks to Calla Van Atta and Nia Franklin for their beautiful smiles on the last page. Thanks to Jeff Croff for the challenging role as Clifford Berryman, and thanks to Jim Redmond who worked his bear dogs for me.

A special thanks to Stella Marie and Karl Barathy for acting out numerous scenes as Rose and Morris Michtom. Thanks to Dr. Jim Sikarskie and his horse Sadie for truly getting into their roles as Theodore Roosevelt and Manitou. Bully for you!

Finally to Heather Hughes, my editor, who has given her all for this book.

— Gijsbert van Frankenhuyzen

In the days when America was a younger country
and much of the land was filled with dense green forests,
animals roamed freely through the great American wilderness.

In the cities, the clip-clop of horses' feet could be heard as they pulled black buggies through bustling streets. Smoking black trains rolled across the countryside connecting cities and towns to prairies and forests, moving travelers across the wild territories of America.

In those days there lived a strong,
adventurous man with a big, bushy mustache.
He was the President of the United States of America,
and his name was Theodore Roosevelt.
The people of America adored their President
and they fondly called him "Teddy".

Teddy Roosevelt loved adventures. He loved to go exploring while riding on his horse, Manitou. Teddy wandered through the wooded valleys of Pennsylvania and climbed the towering peaks of the Colorado Rockies. He roamed the sweeping green prairies, marveling at nature's beauty. But one of the things Teddy loved to do the most was camp in the wide-open spaces of America and fall asleep under a blanket of a thousand twinkling stars.

Teddy often rode on Manitou while hunting wild animals. In those days, many Americans hunted deer and bears. Teddy loved hunting too. During one trip, Teddy traveled to the states of Mississippi and Louisiana. The two states wanted this great and fair man to settle an argument about a boundary line. When his work was done, he decided to explore the green forests of Mississippi and go bear hunting.

Late in the day, on November 14, 1902, as the sun was setting, some of the men in the president's group cornered a young bear. Barking dogs surrounded the frightened bear, as the men roped and tied it to a tree.

One of the men cried out, "President Roosevelt! Come quick! We have a bear for you!"

Branches cracked and twigs snapped as President Roosevelt raced Manitou through the thick forest. Hearing the excited voices of his men, he reached the clearing where the men and barking dogs were gathered. All were pointing at a bear that had been roped and tied to a tree. The frightened bear clawed at the rope, trying to free itself. The bear whipped his head back and forth. Its back feet kicked up clouds of dust and dirt.

Teddy looked down at his rifle and then...
laid it on the ground. He shouted out to his men,
"Stop badgering that bear! It is helpless. Let it go!"
Following the president's orders the men cut the rope
and let the bear go free.

A few days later a newspaper cartoonist named
Clifford Berryman heard about the president's meeting with the bear.
He drew a cartoon illustrating President Roosevelt and a wild bear.
The cartoon first appeared in a newspaper called *The Washington Post*.
People everywhere were talking about how the president had ordered his
men to let a wild bear go free. Soon, the cartoon appeared in newspapers
all over the country. People from New York to Michigan to California saw the
cartoon and read about Teddy's kindness toward the defenseless bear.
The nation's love for their president grew even stronger.

A couple from New York, Rose and Morris Michtom, saw the cartoon while reading their morning newspaper and, like so many other people of America, were touched by what President Roosevelt had done.

Rose and Morris owned a candy shop. They loved having children visit their shop. Big glass jars, stuffed full of brightly colored candy, lined the shelves. The smell of peppermint and lemon drops and licorice sticks filled the air. There were shelves with porcelain dolls, shelves with wooden toy soldiers, and shelves with windup toy trains.

Rose and Morris talked about their president's kindness as they prepared to open their candy shop that morning. As they talked about the bear in the cartoon, an idea for a new toy was born. Rose and Morris thought children might like a soft, cuddly toy. Something a child could squeeze and hug while drifting off to sleep. They decided to make a stuffed toy bear.

Rose and Morris both agreed that a soft, furry material the color of golden honey would be perfect. Morris skillfully cut out the pattern for each little limb and paw. He cut out patterns in the shape of a bear's head and body and then handed them to Rose.

Rose always enjoyed sewing and sat quietly humming as she sewed the pieces together. She tenderly filled each part with fluffy stuffing. Each limb was attached to the body with a special metal wheel that was hidden under the golden fur. Just like a real bear, this toy bear's legs could move. Rose gently held the little bear's paw as she checked to see that each little limb moved up, down, and all the way around.

Next, Rose used shiny black
boot buttons for the eyes. As she
delicately sewed black thread into
the honey fur, forming a little nose
and a mouth, Rose's eyes sparkled just like
the boot-button eyes of her new little bear. Rose nuzzled her
face against the golden honey fur and thought, "you, little
bear, will make a child very, very happy."

The next morning, Rose awoke early and began to make
another toy bear. As she sat touching the soft fur, Rose
imagined how wonderful it would be if all the children in
the world could have their own special bear.

Rose and Morris excitedly placed the two stuffed bears in
the front window of their candy shop. They smiled proudly
at their two golden-colored bears as people passing by stopped
and admired their new creations.

The little bears didn't sit very long in the candy shop window though. Before the end of the day, both bears had a new home.

While Morris was closing up the candy store that evening he suddenly realized they needed a name for their toy bears. What would be a good name? Hmmm!!! Teddy's Bear, he thought.

Morris wondered if their adventurous president would mind if they named their toy bears, "Teddy's Bear". Morris thought the proper thing to do would be to ask the president if he minded, so he decided to write him a letter. In the letter, Morris told the president how Mr. Berryman's cartoon had inspired him and his wife to create two toy bears and how the children loved them. Morris told him how they were going to make more soft, cuddly bears, but they needed a name for them. Morris asked the president if they could use his name.

While Morris was writing the letter, Rose began making another bear to escort the letter to the White House. Stitch by stitch, Rose carefully sewed the bear. While she was stitching the little bear, Morris thought of something. "Rose, I believe our little messenger should dress up for such an important trip!" Morris thought a vest would be very proper for a White House visit and Rose agreed. Rose cut out and sewed a little leather vest. Next, she slipped the fancy vest onto the bear's little body. Then she fastened a small gold chain from one vest pocket to a buttonhole. It looked like their bear was wearing a pocket watch, just like President Roosevelt.

Now, the little bear looked ready for the White House. Their hearts and minds filled with excitement as they gingerly placed the letter and the bear into a box. Rose and Morris addressed the package to:

President Theodore Roosevelt
The White House
Washington D.C.

Rose and Morris worried that a busy man like the President of the United States wouldn't have time to answer a letter about a toy bear.

Day after day, week after week, Rose and Morris waited for a reply. They eagerly searched their mail for a letter from the president. Finally, one day they received an envelope from the White House. Morris's hands trembled as he opened the envelope. Rose's heart pounded. Inside they found a handwritten letter from President Theodore Roosevelt! Nervously, Morris read the letter aloud.

"Dear Mr. and Mrs. Michtom:
I warmly thank you for your letter and the fine stuffed bear you made. I can hardly wait to show my children. However, I don't think my name is likely to be worth much in the toy bear business, but you are welcome to use it. I wish you great luck with your toy bear business.
Sincerely,
Theodore Roosevelt"

The president loved the little bear, and he approved of the name!

Thereafter, Rose and Morris proudly named each bear "Teddy's Bear". It wasn't long before little girls and boys were enjoying their very first stuffed bears, made with love by Rose and Morris, in honor of a great president.

Millions and millions of children all around the world
have since held on tightly to their teddy bears.
A teddy bear is a trusted, faithful, and timeless friend
whose dedication is always ready and never-ending.